Unlocking Kung Fu
A Comprehensive Guide for Beginners

Unlocking Kung Fu
A Comprehensive Guide for Beginners

by Noah Knapp

 Turtle Press   Santa Fe

To contact the author or to order additional copies of this book:
call 1-800-778-8785 or visit www.TurtlePress.com

ISBN 978-1-934903-06-3
LCCN 2008020549
Printed in the United States of America

10 9 8 7 6 5 4 3 2 1 0

Library of Congress Cataloguing in Publication Data

Knapp, Noah.
Unlocking kung fu : a comprehensive guide for beginners / by Noah Knapp.
   p. cm.
ISBN 978-1-934903-06-3
1. Kung fu. I. Title.
GV1114.7.K63 2008
796.815'9--dc22
                                                2008020549

The author would like to extend special thanks to:

Master Kishore Hiranand

Carolina Hiranand

Mymuse Gayle-Macron

Dan Biales

Alex Harris

&

Sifu Brian Knapp

Contents

Introduction

Kung fu is for everyone. Artistic, beneficial for body and mind, useful in defense; Kung Fu is all of these things and more, however there is one thing that Kung Fu is NOT: Kung Fu is NOT beyond anyone's reach. The purpose of this book is to take you inside the workings of Kung Fu training techniques and reveal the so-called "secrets of the art."

As many instructors of Kung Fu would tell you, the art is not necessarily difficult, it is simply comprised of movements that you wouldn't naturally come up with yourself. Kung Fu is not magic either. It should always be remembered that Kung Fu is simply the result and effectiveness of comprehensive study; the same study that you are now engaged in.

Kung Fu stylists utilize certain key practices that give them their imposing edge; a system of movements which may seem almost impossibly efficient. Due to the fact that these covert movements are changed only slightly from the norm, most of the time no one can even see the difference. One of my best students claimed that Kung Fu is the art of millimeters. What he meant is that while our covert practices produce an enormous difference to the effectiveness of a technique, the alterations from standard movements are minute at best. Herein lies the purpose of this book. Every chapter will reveal these seemingly covert practices within "key boxes".

Inside these marked boxes you will find the "secretive" knowledge or "hidden" practices of the techniques. These are the very same mysterious applications that masters have utilized for thousands of years.

By following simple rules and guidelines, Kung Fu practitioners hold themselves among the top ranking martial artists today. How? What our stylists strive to achieve is nothing more than the removal of common mistakes that are regularly performed by common persons. Therefore, the goal of this guide is not only to educate and inform, but also to dispel and remove the mystery and misconceptions that commonly surround this art.

One thing should be kept in mind more than anything else throughout these pages; Kung Fu is totally attainable by anyone. You are simply recreating "muscle memory."

Consider the concept of muscle memory to be a second nature, like sleep walking; your body just performs actions that it is used to although unconscious of its actions.

But what of the Kung Fu portrayed in movies? Is that what you are supposed to be in the pursuit of? Is it as difficult as it looks? Is it even real? For the most part, yes, but it is as true to revealing the Kung Fu you would use in combat as Bugs Bunny is to revealing a real rabbit. Most techniques you see in the cinema are more representative of Wushu, a style of gymnastic Kung Fu. The moves in these films are usually performed by acrobatic experts, glamorized in their production, and choreographed to be as large and stunning as possible. Try to consider that the moves you see on the silver screen are merely based off of practical Kung Fu techniques.

You must remember that Kung fu is as much science as it is anything else; Physics mixed with physiology. As these are areas of science, there are rules that must be appreciated. However it is within these rules, the rules that reign over all human beings, that you will find your advantage. Try to think about Kung Fu as chess rather than to equate it with being a superman. The better player should always win. **Strength, Size, & Speed are not unconquerable; Skill can master them all.** However, the goal of this book is not to make you an expert. It is to introduce you to the possibilities that Kung Fu offers.

We are going to start from scratch, assuming no previous knowledge. There are three very equal and important reasons for this.

1) "Basic" knowledge may be common to some and completely foreign to others.

2) Previous knowledge may be inaccurate and need correcting.

3) Even if you know something, it is always advisable to revisit and rethink important lessons, solidifying and reinforcing your training.

Using the strategies and training techniques in this book will take you right inside the inner workings of the style. The insight within will help you understand that truly anyone can utilize this art and perform all aspects of it with great success while greatly improving their own ability.

History of Training

Many stories have emerged about the origins of Kung Fu. Some would believe that a Chinese priest was walking by a pond one day and observed the movements of a crane fighting a snake and therefore created the roots of modern day Kung Fu. Others would assure that a revered prince created manuals of contemplation and study for monks after almost a decade of exile at a shaolin temple. Still more would date it back to a Chinese army general who devised study and method to train his troops. Any and all of these accounts may be true.

In truth, Kung Fu's origins date back thousands of years and have certainly been skewed over the ages. All was not lost though through the passage of time. For the most straightforward answer we need only look at the meaning and translation of "Kung Fu."

Kung Fu directly means, "to be skilled or adept at." However it does not specify exactly the manner in which one would be trained in. In later years scholars have assumed that "Kung Fu" meant that one was proficient in the branches of many of martial arts. The fact of the matter is that Kung Fu now, no matter what the original intention, is assumed to mean proficiency defending one's self.

It is assumed that the first regular practitioners of Kung Fu were undoubtedly soldiers, trained to defend their domain, but as years passed the wars ended, these soldiers returned to their homes and over time handed the knowledge down to their children. When the necessity arose, these descendents subsequently drew from that original knowledge and utilized whatever they could to successfully protect themselves. These people were no longer fighting experts, but rather more likely farmers defending themselves, their families, or lands. What they had is what you will gain by reading this book, the keys to past knowledge, studies of movement, motion, and the human body. These persons partook of wisdom that had been handed to them over many generations, that which is now being handed to you.

The generalized term "Kung Fu" leaves one to believe that it is merely a single art, but throughout the many years changes and adaptations took place. Knowledge was passed down from teacher (or "Sifu") to student over and over again and with every individual, each school left it's own indelible mark on the principal foundation. Happily, this is still the case today and for many more generations Kung Fu will evolve and grow.

It is true that in each school you will find varying points of view over things from artistic vs. practical applications, all the way to uniform preferences and on which side is it proper to tie the knot on your sash. However the main differences now are observed in two separate ways: Northern vs. Southern and Internal vs. External. The Key Box at right explains this in more detail.

Arguments can be leveled about the superiority of each style, but it should be remembered that, however different the many unique styles of Kung Fu may seem, they all branch from the same foundation. Try to consider the variances in style as you would doctors specializing in different fields of medicine. While they each have considerable differences in specialization, they still all had to become the basic "doctor" first. Every physician had to attain the same central knowledge from which they draw their expertise before they could become specialists in advanced fields. Fortunately, it is a basic foundation, the core of Kung Fu, which we are now about to study.

There are certain systems, rules, and routines that experienced Kung Fu practitioners rely upon to display and practice the mastery of style that they do. These very same practices will now become yours. Once you have completed study of the material in this book you will have the same knowledge and vocabulary, the identical keys to defense of that these practitioners have used for thousands of years. Kung Fu will no longer be a mysterious and unattainable thing, rather it will take it's place as what we know that most do not. Remember, Kung Fu is nothing more and nothing less than a comprehensive study of the human body.

Kung Fu contains dozens upon dozens of distinctive schools separated by the differences in style, technique, training, and performance. The seemingly endless list of styles may be daunting to look at, but certain key terms and groupings easily clarify so that one anyone understand.

Broken down it looks like this:

Internal styles (Tai Chi Chaun, Bagua Zhang, & Hsing I) concentrate on channeling energy throughout each movement while External styles (Hung Gar, Wing Chun, etc.) rely upon the skill, training, and knowledge of the physical body.

Northern style (Kung Fu - Mandarin translation) mostly emphasizes fluidity and ease of movement also relying heavily on the lower body and legs, while Southern style (Gung Fu - Cantonese translation) tends to lend it's foundations more to concentrating on strong upper body, hand, and arm techniques.

The styles are often named with the keys to understanding what they will be about. The word "Chuan" means Fist. Tai Chi Chuan literally means "Supreme Ultimate Fist." Zhang translates to Palm as in "Bagua Zhang" or "Eight Trigram Palm." Find the translation and the style is usually revealed.

School names are also often used such as Chen and Yang styles of Tai Chi Chuan or Gar meaning the family's style such as in Hung Gar or the Hung Family's school.

Philosophy

It should be remembered that Kung Fu is an art mastered in the mind as well as the body. Your mental prowess is endless, whereas physical attributes are limited. This is where the ever important concepts of philosophy enter in.

Meditation aims for relaxation, inner thought, personal introspection, balance and reflection. It allows for both clarity and a quieting of the mind. Kung Fu philosophy at it's core dictates tranquility; a balance that must be kept in order to assure success. The basic concepts are to remain calm and easy in every situation and to find a balance in every circumstance that presents itself. Here enters the most commonly associated symbol of Kung Fu: the Yin-Yang.

The Yin-Yang is an ancient symbol of completion and balance through duality. It is the blending of give and take, a unity of opposites. Yin and Yang are not only dependant upon each other, but are also part of one another. Once boiled down, the idea is that one side does not exist without the other.

Okay, let's get away from the enigmatic designation of Yin and Yang and get to the real meaning. Sometimes, hard to believe as it is, we can find ourselves the victor by giving our opponent everything they move toward. Yin and Yang teach us that there IS more than one avenue of success. It is about our own balance and that which we share with others. As we must regulate ourselves to remain calm during an altercation, so must we react.

Maintaining the balance is not a difficult concept, if our opponent lays an offense against us, we must react in a way that will nullify the attack. No matter what they do, we must respond in a manner which will invalidate or cancel out the offense.

As we go along in the book, we will recognize that, more than likely, our opponent's movements betray their actual wishes and that we only need to react at the proper time to exploit their weaknesses. Once again, within yourself you will find the keys of recognizing not only the weaknesses of others, but also your own guarantees of success.

First of all you must remember during a confrontation that no matter how difficult it may be at times, return to the knowledge that whatever altercation you find yourself in, regardless of outcome, it will pass. There is darkness and light that can be found in any situation and difficult time are no exception. Truthfully, what Kung Fu is teaching here is no more than relying on one's training and assuming that it will aid in the removal of a negative outcome.

Bowing

Whether performed to show respect or simply to offer a greeting, bowing is an integral part of Kung Fu. It is how we identify each other as Kung Fu practitioners and while style and manner may differ from school to school, there are two very common and basic ways to bow.

Folding Hands

To accurately perform this bow, allow your left hand to cover your right fist. Hold your hands just below your chin and extend slightly away from your body while nodding your head forward. This is the most common and commonly accepted greeting.

Royal Salute

A much more ceremonial way of showing respect, the royal salute is withheld in all but very formal situations. This bow is achieved in five separate steps.

Slide your right foot tight next to your left. At the same time raise your left hand to be held, palm open, high at your shoulder and place the thumb of your right fist directly in front of it. Make certain not to cover your face.

Swing the joined hands down to your right hip, extending your right foot to step slightly forward.

Bring your left foot forward and in tight against your right. Once your feet have met, extend both hands to almost their full reach out in front of you.

Take one step back with both feet, right then left. After your feet have joined, pull your now clenched fists to your hips with the wrists pointing upward.

Finish the bow by bending at the waist.

Insight into Developing Power

Development of true power in kung fu is neither complicated nor is it difficult. Effective training of force is usually achieved with proper practice of the movements, but there are also alternative methods of amplifying your power. However, there is one most important concept that is essential to proper training; Muscle doesn't matter. You must understand that there is a very, very large difference between power and strength.

The basic rules for effective training both promote and maintain a sound being. Therefore, hold in consideration at all times that if it hurts, don't do it. Kung Fu NEVER needs to be painful. Remember that you are practicing systems and techniques that build into your body's memory, you are not training to build muscle. Assuredly, your health, wellness of being, and physique will improve the more you train, but these are side effects of becoming fluent in Kung Fu.

Now let's return to extending and enhancing power. Almost every person on earth has enough power to subdue an adversary, but they simply don't know how to release it. To illustrate this best, consider a hallway with a series of doors. Every door is a joint and just as if you lock a door, locking a joint will allow nothing through. Always keeping your joints bent is not only an issue of safety and structure, it can also be an important aspect of channeling power. Leaving the completion of your power to fall outward is of utmost importance. Here enters the concept of floppy not sloppy.

When throwing your energy outward from your center you must remember to maintain as much control over you body as possible. Let your strikes to fall through their furthest extent, but always retain the knowledge that they must return for another issuance. When allowing the body to fall through the completion of it's force you must remember not to overextend yourself to the point of vulnerability. Your actions should always fall within the realm of your own control, however untamed they may seem in action. As the fluidity of your movement increases, so too will your natural force be amplified along with it.

Below are three, usually undisclosed, methods in which Kung Fu increases it's power. Due to their extreme effectiveness, these practices have each merited special mention within a key box. Simple practice of the movements contained within this book will aid and enhance your output of true force.

Hip Twisting

Though it is always best to keep your shoulders facing your opponent, it is well known in Kung Fu that all of your real power should come from your hips. The basic swiveling action of your hips during a strike will increase your power tenfold if not more. Even a simple jab is turned into quite an onslaught by including the torque power of your midsection. This method of attacking gives the power of not only legs to your strike, but adds, most importantly, the force of torque and rotation from your hips.

Example of Hip Twist

Remembering to keep your shoulders forward during your attack, begin your strike.

Leave your assault forward, increasing your force by twisting your hips away from the inception point of the strike.

Swivel your hips completely to the other side as you finish your attack.

Spine Waves

Why hit someone with only the strength in your hand when you can just as easily hit them with power held in your entire body. Here enter spine waves.

An important and usually imperceptible practice within Kung Fu, spine waves allow users to cause a huge upsurge of energy within them. After basically pushing into the ground, the practitioner channels the pressure throughout the body, adding to the force with every muscle it passes through and releasing it only once it has reached the hand. The definition may seem complicated, but their performance is fairly simple in practice.

Begin in a straight posture.

To start the spine wave, extend your knees forward ahead of you.

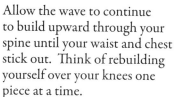

3

4

Allow the wave to continue to build upward through your spine until your waist and chest stick out. Think of rebuilding yourself over your knees one piece at a time.

Lastly, just as you are about to fall forward, allow the entire pressure of the wave to exit through your arms and out of your hands (as a punch or palm strike during an altercation.)

Using Gravity

Gravity is a stronger force than any power attained by humans. This technique allows you to lay the maximum amount of force upon your opponent, not just the mere strength of your punch. To utilize this falling power all one needs to do is yield to the external forces around us. Regardless of the strike chosen, (punch, kick, head butt, etc.), by slightly buckling our knees forward upon or directly before the point of impact, we force the entire weight of our body into the hit. Arching your strike ensures that you use your entire body to hit, not just the appendage with which you make contact to your opponent. Remember that timing is essential.

Begin by starting a standard punch (practices discussed in a later chapter).

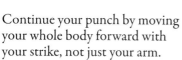

Continue your punch by moving your whole body forward with your strike, not just your arm.

Lastly, you will complete your attack by falling slightly forward at the very moment you allow your strike to peak.

Summary of Developing Power

Start off slowly in these force exercises. Be patient and build up speed over time. As with everything else in Kung Fu, your timing and performance will improve the more you practice. Keep in mind, the simple act of performing the moves will actively develop and increase your power with each session of training.

Study of Circles, Curves, & Arcs

The structure of a strong foundation is crucial to the application of proper Kung Fu techniques. Circles, curves, and arcs are used for the cycling and recycling of energy instead of stopping and starting it over and over again. These practices allow for perfect efficiency, lessen fatigue, and aid in continuous control over our bodies.

Our bodies are not two dimensional and as such cannot be best protected with the usage of straight stances. Also while straight hits may be quicker, they are not as strong. Think of baseball. Major league players swing their bats in a curved manner toward the ball for the mightiest hits, they only push the bat straight forward to the ball for a tiny hit called a bunt.

The properly curved structure of our bodies is not only a perfect foundation. Truthfully, many of the benefits of standing and holding in bent lines are for the protection of our own being.

Consider again that same long hallway with a series of doors all along the way. Each door is a joint and energy **needs** to get through or it risks being trapped inside. Locking a joint is like locking a door, all the energy will get trapped *at that joint* and not be able to exit. Keeping the joints bent assures that if a strike is landed, no force damage or hyperextension is possible.

Ward Off Position (Front)   ## Ward off (Side)

Above is a standard "Warding Off Position." Practice of this positioning will be discussed in later chapters. The purpose here is only to notice how the curved structure of the body leads the weight out to the sides and into a more fortified and even dispersion. The same is true of the arms when accepting force and channeling that energy down through the body. However, in utilizing arced lines, you not only create for a more fortified formation, but you allow yourself to move within the natural structure of the body. Locking joints can equal assured hyperextension and all but guarantee long term injury, while curves grant extra room to avoid hyperextension.

Absorbing our opponent's energy, whether manipulating their power or accepting a blow, utilizes the science of curved structures. Under distress, a straight line will break at it's weak point, whereas a properly positioned arc will simply force weight onto itself to hold strong. Architecture has regularly utilized arches and curved foundations for just this reason since ancient times.

The practice of curves, arcs, and circles during training is very simple. The idea is basically that once you expend energy, you do not end it, you simply recycle it. The reasons for this are numerous, but include never offering a force that you yourself cannot control. Whether expending or accepting an assault, cycling the attack will insure that you will never find yourself unable to maintain the force. Also, bending your attacks allows for constant movement. This leaves your blows to blend into each other instead of stopping and reissuing each time you wish to deliver a strike.

The concept of these ideas may seem a bit confusing at first, but with even slight practice you will see how truly easy it can be and that this is indeed how your body wants to move.

Below are outlined proper manners in which you can train your body's muscle memory to find the path of least resistance using the aforementioned curves, arcs, and circles.

Recycling Practice

Your attacker throws a strike at you.

After accepting the strike you blend the force off to your side.

Once the strength of the attack has been spent, cycle the force of the attack down in a circular manner.

Continue the circular movement forward and away from you.

Once the attacker's force is cycled completely, you may reissue their force directly back at them.

Examples of training this and other energy recycling techniques will be detailed in the "Training Drills" chapter.

It is very important to ALWAYS stretch before practicing any training system. Due to the specific nature of our training, certain stretches are considered mandatory. Herein are listed those stretches that Kung Fu stylists utilize in order to ready themselves properly.

Preparation is very important. Remember rule number one: Safety first. Even if you have spent time stretching earlier in the day, do it again. Stretching not only prepares the body for a workout, but also greatly reduces the risk of injury at the same time. The few simple movements listed hereafter take little time to perform and will assure a healthy training program.

Do not push yourself too hard! Your opponents and training partners are not the only ones who can cause injury to you. You may bring yourself just as great of a risk by demanding too much of your body too soon. Be patient as you progress through your education. You will find that you are becoming more limber and that your range of comfortable extension will increase over time. However, pushing yourself too hard may cause injury that actually delays your natural progression. Never pull a stretch further than is comfortable for you or past the range of your "natural torque."

Natural Torque

Natural torque is a subject usually tackled when talking about "Chin Na," or body locks and manipulation, but it important to understand it in the context of stretches as well. Each of the joints in the body have a preset limit as to range of motion and mobility. The maximum scope of joint extension without injury is known as "natural torque."

While the goal in Chin Na is to proceed past your opponent's range, the ambition for it's applications in stretching are far less. Slowly and carefully find the natural torque in each joint. Make sure you are fully stretching, but not over-extending each time. Once you believe you have found the maximum, yet comfortable extension, hold it for a minimum of 10 seconds. The ease of finding your own personal range will increase with time and practice.

As was stated previously, regular use of this application will safely extend your muscles and avoid painful strains and pulls. With time, both your muscles and your tendons will expand, increasing your range.

Remember the golden rule - If it hurts, you're doing it wrong.

Total Body Stretches

While it is recommended to perform common stretches such as calf and quadriceps stretches, practice in Kung Fu necessitates a bit more. Due to the usage of less common joints and muscles, additional bodily preparation must be observed. The following stretches have been devised with Kung Fu practice and training in mind and will aid you in properly readying yourself.

NOTE: To adequately prepare your body, it is best to start at your core and work your way out to the extremities.

1. Full Body Circles

Make a pyramid with your hands. Extend your arms to their fullest extent and stare straight up. Keeping your arms completely stretched to the completion of their range, and circle your body downward from your waist to either side. Attempt to run your hands over the top of your feet and across as you continue moving. Complete the stretch by returning to the top in the same manner in which you began. Make certain to perform the stretch both clockwise and counter-clockwise.

Recommended repetitions: 2-3 times.

2. Hip Twists

Crossing your arms in front of you, grab onto your opposite shoulders. Turn your knees inward to avoid unwanted strain. Keeping your elbows tightly at your sides, begin to rotate your hips from side to side. Do not start off too fast or hard! Begin slowly and increase as your comfort dictates.

Recommended repetitions: 10-15 times.

Arm, Wrist, & Hand Stretches

3. Outside Shoulder Pulls

Move your left hand across the right shoulder. With you right hand reach up from underneath the left arm. Once contact has been made, pull slightly, extending the range. Make certain to perform stretch on both shoulders.

Recommended repetitions: 2 times on each side

4. Shoulder Circles

Extend your arms directly out to your sides until your elbows are almost straight. Point your fingers as far outward as is comfortably possible. Begin by making small forward circles from the shoulders. It is recommended that you slowly increase the size of your circle as you perform them until you are rotating to the full span of your range. Once you have completed the exercise forward, perform in the same manner with backward circles.

Recommended repetitions: 15-20 times for each direction.

5. Palm Press

Place your palms completely together. Making sure to keep *complete* and firm contact, and gently press inward and downward, holding for intervals of 10-15 seconds.

Recommended repetitions: 5-10 times.

6. Back Wrist Touch

Raising your elbows high at your side, place the backs of your hands together at the knuckles. Try to keep close contact at the wrist as you gently press your elbows downward.

Recommended repetitions: 5-10 times.

7. Outside Wrist Twist

 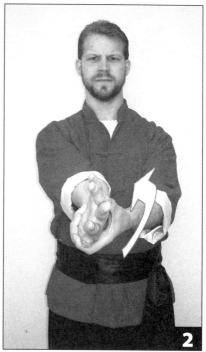

Stare directly at the palm of your right hand, holding it no more than 8 inches from your face. Circle your left hand around from the outside and grab the right thumb from behind.

Once thumb has been grabbed, extend both hands outward until both arms straighten and a comfortable stretch in the wrist has been achieved.

Recommended repetitions: 2 time on each side.

8. Inside Wrist Twist

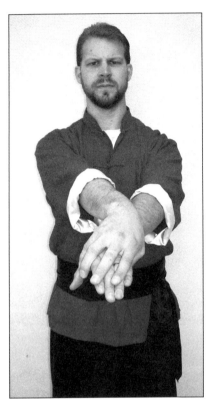 

Hold your left hand, palm down directly in front of you. Place your right hand over the top, grabbing the outside of the left hand with your thumb.

Gently roll the left hand over until a comfortable stretch in the wrist has been achieved.

Recommended repetitions: 2 times on each side.

9. Wrist Circling

Extend your arm outward from your body and circle your wrist over and over at the furthest comfortable extent.

Recommended repetitions: 25-30 times on each side.

Leg and Foot Stretches

10. Butterfly Stretch

Sit on the ground and place the bottoms of your feet together.

Grasp your hands together over your toes and lean forward, pulling slightly as you move forward. Hold for 10 seconds before releasing. After each repetition, pull your feet in closer to you.

Recommended repetitions: 2-3 times.

11. Ankle Circles

Raise each foot slightly off of the ground and circle it outward at first and then inward.

Recommended repetitions: 5 times in each direction.

Neck Stretches

12. Single Neck Stretches

Stare straight upward, feeling the stretch in the front of your neck and throat.

Continue by turning your head full to the left, feeling the stretch full on the right side of your neck.

Next touch your chin to your chest, feeling the stretch at the back of your neck.

Turn completely to the right, feeling the stretch on the left side of your neck.

Lastly, gently clasp your hands over the back of your head. DO NOT PULL DOWN! Simply allow the weight of your arms to give additional stretching. Pulling may risk a series of pulled neck muscles.

Make certain to hold in each direction until you feel that your neck has been properly extended and is prepared for a workout.

Recommended repetitions: As needed

13. Neck Rotations

Turn your head entirely to your right. Circle around several times and then circle in the other direction.

Recommended repetitions: As needed, but no fewer than 5 times in each direction.

14. Shake Out

Stand up and shake out your core and limbs. This will aid in releasing any remaining tightened muscles after the stretches you have just performed.

Recommended repetitions: As needed.

Chapter Summary

Once you have completed the routine, remember that your body will regularly tell you what you need. If for some reason you feel the need to revisit any stretch, by all means, do it before you proceed to your workout.

SECTION THREE
Preparation and Positioning

Body Preparation

Some rules must be observed for proper body preparation. First and foremost is the rule that safety must come before anything else. Knowing this, there are three parts of proper body preparation in Kung Fu and they **must** be followed in order. First relax, next, and then, most importantly, relax, lastly, relax. Hopefully the point has been made clear and no other wasted ink is necessary.

No matter the area of preparation, make certain that ALL joints are loose and unlocked. This should be a constant throughout all of your training. The reasons for this are numerous at minimum. It is easiest to understand by considering drunk driving accidents. Studies have shown that drunken drivers regularly survive accidents that their victims do not. Why is this? The answer : is quite simple; being drunk creates a sense of relaxation throughout the entire body. When the impact occurs, the force is more easily dissipated through a relaxed body.

The remainder of this section contains further detail of proper body positioning.

Whole Body Positioning

Seated Relax Position

Not all positions in Kung Fu deal with confrontation. The seated relax position is regularly used during training to rest, align your body, and to center your mind. To perform this position, sit with your back straight and legs crossed. Allow the inside of your wrists to rest on and over your knees. Keeping this posture allows perfect structure and aids in breathing and relaxation.

Hand & Arm Positioning

The hands and arms bear much of the responsibility of accepting and controlling aggressive force. As has been previously stated, the use of arcs in your structure will dissipate energy through you, but remember mostly to relax your muscles and joints, allowing for no tension or resistance within yourself.

Ward off (front)	**Ward off (side)**

Your hands and arms should remain relaxed and extended in front of you, as if pressing slightly away from your body. Elbows should be kept near the sides and pointed downward to aid in proper striking and to allow for proper protection of the midsection.

Leg, Foot, & Knee Positioning

Preparing yourself for varying height of attacks will become an important part of your preparation. Special consideration should be given when considering bends originating from the lower body. One of the biggest mistakes that an individual can perform during training is to lower themselves by bending at the waist. When bending forward, a myriad of faults can occur ranging from loss of balance, control, range of motion, mobility, etc. Lowering yourself from your knees not only allows for uninterrupted balance, but also helps to control your ability to protect yourself. As has been stated previously, a slight bend in your knees is highly recommended for joint safety. It only makes sense to continue this practice for ongoing body safety during an attack.

As far as consideration of our feet and ankles, a standard inward turn to the feet will provide not only the ever important stability, but also allow us the range of full turns from our hips without tearing at muscles and ligaments in our legs when throwing strikes.

Ward off (front)

Ward off (side)

Spine, Neck, & Torso

Ward off (Side)

Preparation of your spine, neck, and torso are very easy, but remember that this region of your body contains all of the things that keep you whole and alive. The spine is naturally curved and not straight in design. Leave your back and neck relaxed at all time, however be certain that your are completely upright. Crunching your body forward can restrict breathing and blood flow. Make sure that your head is held high. Consider it to be the antenna of your whole body.

Stances

It is difficult to explain the importance of stances. Not that they are of such importance that mere words cannot describe their worth, but rather that understanding their necessity is a complex concept to appreciate. Stances help you structure your body so that it can transition from position to position properly. They promote balance, ease of movement, and aid in correctly aligning the composition of your body.

While it is true that stances are a very integral part of Kung Fu, it should not be assumed that their arduous practice is essential to the start your training. As has been stated previously, differences in style will dictate exact positioning during advanced technique and stance styles may vary greatly between schools.

The idea is to utilize your training and build a strong foundation with steady training in the stances listed below. When first beginning your stance training, start easy, holding no stance for more than 1 minute. As time passes and endurance improves, raise the duration you hold each stance. Minding your comfort level, build up each stance to around 10 minutes; anything more may be considered excessive. In standing properly for the recommended amount of time, you create muscle memory. These stances will become your default setting, leaving your body ready to find comfort and ease in the proper positions during the rest of your training, not to mention when a crucial moment of self-defense arises.

Below are 10 "foundation" stances, or rather stances that are very common and found in many types of Kung Fu. Despite the fact that names and specifics of positioning may differ, most styles of kung fu include the following as basic postures.

Ready Ward Off (side)

The "ready" ward off is very similar to the previously described standard ward off position with few changes. If desiring a "ready" stance (one prepared for confrontation,) allow one foot to extend slightly forward ahead of you, making sure the matching hand is the higher hand. Ex. If your *left* foot braces forward, make certain your *left* hand is held as the high hand.

Horse Stance

The best manner in which to describe the horse stance to imagine yourself riding a horse. Spread your feet out past your shoulders. Bend your knees forward to absorb pressure. Turn your closed fists until your wrists point upward and pull them close into your hips.

Bow Stance

The upper body of the Bow Stance is achieved in the same manner as the horse stance. Pull your upturned wrists tight into the waist. Step forward with either leg, leaving the other to drag behind. Bend the front knee forward, extending the back leg in a straight line.

Long Fist

The long fist extends the range of your strike to it's fullest extent. Let your punching arm reach as far as is possible (remembering to keep a slight bend at all times.) Make certain your free hand guards your midsection. Pull your back leg up and brace it against the inside of the knee on the standing leg for balance.

Drawing the Sword

Drawing the sword creates a straight line for energy to pass through your body. To perform this stance, stick your arms straight out at your side like an airplane. Tip to the sides and extend your leg out forward ahead of you, guarding your knee with the lower hand. With your opposite hand, reach back and up as if drawing a sword high above your head. Bend your free knee back and away, lowering the entirety of your body down.

Receiving Stance

The receiving stance is achieved by extending you hands out forward and up ahead of you. Imagine that you are resting a giant bowl on your chest and holding it with your arms. Palms should be faced upward. Leave one foot to fall forward, bending it slightly at the knee.

Wandering Dragon

Wandering Dragon is as Kung Fu as Kung Fu gets. Step one foot forward ahead of the other, keeping the legs tight and bent at the knee. Turn your hips and torso away to the side, extending both hands outward away from you.

Lotus Nymph

Cross your wrists in front of your eyes and raise them slightly upward. Just as with the ward off and every other stance and position, step forward with the same foot as the high hand. If the right hand is held high, the right foot is meant to move forward under it.

Cat Stance

Nimbly walks the cat. Bend both knees, leaving one foot to extend forward, touching only the ball of your foot and toes on the ground in front of you. Leave the majority of the weight on the back leg. Extend your hands forward in twin snake strikes (detailed in later chapters), one held ahead of you and the other at the elbow of the other.

Iron Staff

Imagine holding a heavy bag of grain over your right shoulder to properly achieve the iron staff. Position yourself the same as you would brace the weight on your shoulder, supporting it overhead with your hand. Leaving your left arm down, bend and extend the elbow slightly away from you, lifting the same knee up to meet this arm at the back of the hand. Brace the left foot on the inside of the right leg's knee.

Coordinating Areas of Blocks

There are several ways to stop an attacker from striking you; different methods for different situations. To be completely confident over each and every area of your body, you must regulate the defense and strengthening of each location. By doing so you will guarantee efficiency and control of your defense. With every possibility of protection, so is there an answer as to the proper manner of security, both defensive and offensive.

Elements of proper offensive and defensive blocking practice are detailed below.

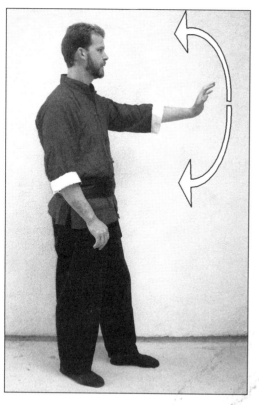

Personal Range
(Upper Body)

This picture shows the range of your arm's possible defense.

Personal Range (Lower Body)

This picture displays the acceptable range of your feet and legs in a confrontation.

Efficiency of Blocking Practice

Blocking efficiency is vital for proper form and foundation. Large expenditures of energy should be considered wasteful and unnecessary. There are several manners in which to best utilize the spending of your actions. Each of the following blocking types are quite different and can be successfully performed in various situations.

Why take your arms far from your body to block a punch when you can achieve the same result by blocking only one inch past your form? By restraining your actions close to your body you force your opponent to bridge the distance. In throwing a punch, you leave them to take up the majority of time covering the void. This will allow a greater reaction time on your part as well as forcing the attacker to expend more energy over the extent of the fight. See the examples that follow.

Blocking Efficiency (Necessary Distance)

The necessary distance for blocking a strike is only one inch past your form.

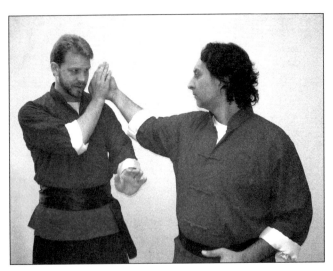

Total safety from the strike is achieved with limited movement.

Blocking Efficiency (Reuse of Blocking hand)

Your opponent throws a strike at you.

The block is pushed to the side.

As the second strike is initiated, we find that the closest blocking hand is, in fact, the just previously used hand.

Maximizing efficiency, the second strike is controlled with the same hand.

Once the second strike has been nullified, your unused hand is free and ready to make a successful attack.

Defensive Blocks

Straight Blocks

There are four basic blocking areas in Kung Fu: up, in, out & down. Overall these four basic areas will more than adequately defend you. Each of the blocks uses the straight extension of your arm's length to protect from an attack, but here is the Kung Fu insight to a more perfect result. If your arm is going to extend away from your body, it is best to do so toward your opponent, keeping your guard in front of you as opposed to spent completely at your side.

The four standard areas are listed as follows:

Upward Block

The standard upward block is accomplished by rising your arm upward underneath the striking arm of your opponent. Use the free hand to guard low on your ribcage, preventing secondary hits. Remember, just because you have blocked one strike doesn't mean another isn't coming!

Inward Block

To achieve an accurately performed inward block, press the inside of your hand or wrist against the outside of the attacking arm. Twist your hips once contact is made and simply let the attacking arm continue past you. Try to keep the elbow of your blocking hand near your side for additional protection.

Outward Block

A proper outward block is attained by using the outside of your wrist, hand, or forearm to push the assault away from the center of your body. Notice once again how the exposed ribcage is blocked with the free hand.

Downward Block

Downward blocks need only timing and gravity to be achieved. Simply let your hand fall and cover your opponent's strike, this time leaving your free hand to maintain the safety of your upper torso and face.

Okay, here's what we're doing that you are not. Most people recognize these four areas of defense, but leave their arms to work as a straight and unbending unit. By hooking your wrist outward or inward depending on the angle of attack, you force a much greater amount of control. Turning your wrists in this manner creates more friction with the attacking appendage and funnels the attack into a limited path instead of letting it simply brush off to any free direction. Also, as has been stated before during discussion of yin and yang, it is not only okay, but it is advisable to yield a little to the strike. This action will leave them slightly off of their balance and allow you to further envelope them into your control.

Moreover, use this simple formula for additional safe coverage: Utilize **both** hands during a block. If one hand is moved high, the other should be moved low and vice versa. This will assure accurate and even defensive coverage over your complete form.

Offensive Blocks

Choke and Stopper Blocks

Choking and stopper blocks fall within an altogether different system of hindering your attacker's movement. Consider the possibility of finding yourself deep within your attacker's striking path. All is not lost in this situation. If you find that the attacking hand is too difficult to centrally locate your block upon, simply look further into the starting point of the assault itself. Every punch that comes from your assailant begins at the center of their form. The extension of the strike must travel through the shoulder, the elbow, and then the wrist before it can be imposed upon it's victim. Here is our leverage point. It is entirely feasible to terminate the attack if the foundation of that strike is restricted. What does this mean in layman's terms? The best way to describe the reasoning for this particular style of blocking is to consider the analogy of killing weeds. If you simply snap off the stem of the weed, it can flourish again in no time, but if you attack at the root, the nuisance will be gone forever.

Our defense would concentrate, for example, not upon restricting the attacking hand, but rather at the shoulder, elbow, or even chest at the source of that hand. Of course the same holds true of the knee, hip, or thigh should the attack come from a kick.

One further benefit of utilizing choking or stopper blocks is that by leaving your hands far from your body, you have several opportunities for contact as the strike comes forward at you.

Your opponent readies to strike you.

The strike is thrown.

Just before the attack reaches you, you slam you hand against the inside of the attacking shoulder, choking the entirety of energy from the strike.

Reaction Strikes

"Never pass the face without saying hello." This is an old quote commonly used by martial arts instructors to compound the idea of efficiency and common sense. The purpose of the saying is in blocking an attacker's strike. While you are moving your hand forward to block the punch, you might as well level a strike of your own in the process. If you have to move your body in a certain way, regardless of intent, you'd might as well achieve everything you can with the movement. Efficiency and purpose stand in place of wasted time and missed opportunity.

A proper reaction strike is achieved by slipping inside the arc of an attacker's punch and leveling one of your own. It is very similar in form and function to the previous "Choking or Stopper blocks," but consider it more as a defense with an agenda.

Your opponent readies to strike you.

The strike is thrown.

Just as with the choke/stopper block, you nullify the root of the attack, however, whereas the purpose of the choke block is simply to stop the attack the reaction strike is utilized as a more effective and damaging strike. Land your attack upon the head, neck, or torso of your attacker, making certain to strike on the inside of the attacker's punch. This will hold them at a safe distance and insure that their strike cannot reach it's destination.

Follow Backs

Efficiency without risk. Simple patterns of back and forth. Follow backs are a true example of give and take. This block is based off of simple logic. The expendable distance of your opponent's attack comes from a finite source. Once the attacker has spent their energy forward upon you, they are left with no alternative but to retract it back and start again. As they retrieve their hand to reset their stance or, perhaps, to reissue another strike, simply attach your movement to them. In recoiling, they will now unknowingly bring you within their own guard. The energy you spend on this strike will be multiplied by that of your opponent. By following your attacker's movement, you will effectively achieve complete access for your own attack.

Your opponent readies to strike you.

The strike is thrown.

You accept the punch with an extended blocking arm.

As the attacker readies to withdraw the unsuccessful strike, you ready to follow with your own hand.

Follow the hand all the way back to the attacker's face. The strength of your strike will easily be multiplied by the force of your attacker's withdrawal.

Returning Strikes

Why let your opponent control their attack? One of the best aspects of Kung Fu is the variances in continued blocking practices. It should always be assumed that more needs to be done in every situation. Below are continued blocking practices that offer alternative options. These following concepts are designed not only to successfully defend your body, but as well to gain control from positive defensive tactics as well.

Your opponent readies to strike you.

The strike is thrown.

At the very same instance that the hand is blocked away from you, use your free hand to strike against the attacker.

Lower Body Blocks

You can utilize the same standard upper body blocking practices for high kicks, but for lower body attacks it is best to let your legs take the lead. The easiest and most effective manner in which you can keep your balance and defend yourself is by simply lowering yourself at the knee and leaning into the strike. The reasons for this seemingly impetuous movement are many. First, by leaning into the strike, you negate the possibility for the attack to peak. Secondly, You cut the distance of your opponent and throw them off both rhythm and balance. Thirdly, it works. The effect will leave you injury free and possibly incapacitate your attacker.

Forward Knee Bend

Lean your body down and forward, simply pointing the tip of your knee at the attacking leg. Regardless of actual final location of this strike, you assure your safety and allow a possibly disabling blow upon your opponent.

SECTION FIVE
Upper Body Striking

Areas of Use and the Myriad of Weapons

The purpose of this entire section is to impose upon you the utmost importance of removing preconceived limitations from yourself and from your options. Most people think only of their hands when thinking of the body's weapons, other's sometimes include feet.

Keep an open mind when it comes striking options, both your own attacks to those of your opponent. Let us now consider that anything, any part of your body, even it's weight, could become a weapon.

During a crisis situation, any feasible defense becomes valid. Knowing that these situations do exist and occur frequently, consider why you would wait until such an instance to lend yourself and your training to the absolute of this truth. Kung Fu allows for the contemplation of these predicaments.

Your head, forearms, shoulders, indeed every piece of your body can be used as a weapon. However, while it is best to never exclude any safe manner in which we may level an attack, we must first concentrate on the basic, standard striking rules within the Kung Fu arsenal.

Basic Striking Rules and Techniques

Safety comes first. This rule must be repeated and remembered at all times. To properly achieve safety however, we must not forget the damage that we can deal to ourselves. To be safe from injury incurred during an attack we must observe the proper areas with which we may lay the attack and the hard on soft rules. We will tackle the latter first.

Hard and Soft rules

Let us first define soft and hard. Soft attacks are those in which you strike with a padded surface (i.e. the palm or the bottom of the foot). Hard surfaces are those which utilize bone as the striking point (i.e. the knuckles or the elbow).

Bone is a very, very hard substance. To smash your knuckles against someone's head would be like throwing a punch at a bowling ball. Yes you may hurt the person, but you will incur quite a bit of damage yourself. When attacking bone, it is better to use a softer striking surface, such as your palm.

To best understand all possibilities, consider the following safety outline:

1. Hard surfaces can hit soft surfaces

2. Hard surfaces can NOT hit hard surfaces

3. Soft surfaces can hit soft surfaces

4. Soft surfaces can hit hard surfaces

Proper Areas of Striking

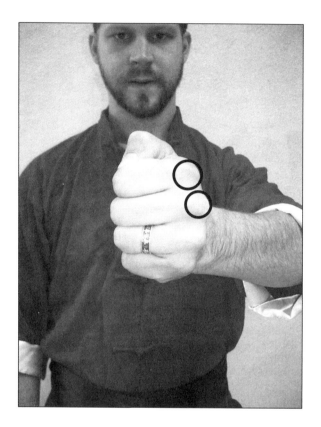

When using a closed fist, regardless of the strike intended, there are only two locations of acceptable striking. The knuckles at the base of the index and middle finger allow for optimal damage to your attacker while offering none back to you. If the same knuckles of the ring and pinky finger are used, the best we can hope for is to only leave ourselves with a minor break.

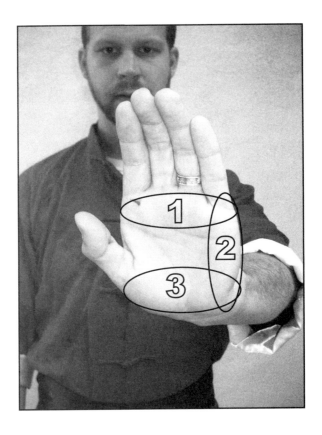

A palm strike offers much more opportunity for varied attack. Three possible strike zones avail themselves upon the inside of our hand.

1. Pad Strike: A sharp and powerful strike can be landed by using the heavily padded area just underneath our fingers.

2. Side Palm: The same area of the hand used to chop. The side of the palm, just underneath the pinky finger, can be used to land quick devastating blows.

3. Heel of the Palm: This area is the essence of a palm strike. Hard, unyielding, forward power that can strike at any surface on your opponent without concern of self-injury.

Basic Hand & Arm Positions

In this section we will cover regularly utilized hand and arm arrangements as well as how they relate to Kung Fu applications. Experts in Kung Fu utilize several positions, each one finding it's use upon the arrival of a unique situation. Below are some of the most common striking practices, including why, how, and in which situations they will best work.

Palm Strike

Seen by many as the best attack possible, the palm strike offers complete safety over an unlimited striking area. Using the flat of your palm, press your hand out and forward anywhere upon your opponent's body. MAKE CERTAIN THAT YOU USE ONLY THE PALM AND NOT FINGERS IN THE ATTACK!

Double Palm Strike

The double palm strike is fashioned in the very same manner as a single palm strike, but is used more as a very strong pressure blow. As with the standard palm strike, throw your hands forward, using only the palm as your striking surface. This attack as well may be used anywhere on the opponent's body.

Press

The press is used for blunt trauma against an opponent. It offers distance as well as a strong offense. To accurately perform it, leave your left arm out in front of you. Turn your palm inward. With your right hand, press against the inside of your raised forearm. The strike zone is the complete back of your left forearm. Use the entirety of your body weight, lunging slightly forward when landing your strike. This strike is best used on the head or torso of your opponent.

Whole Fist

A whole fist is your standing striking punch. To accurately perform it, twist your punch as it moves forward at your opponent. The strike should be completed once the back of the hand is exposed upward. This strike may be landed anywhere on the opponent's body. Remember to use only the striking knuckles of the index and middle fingers.

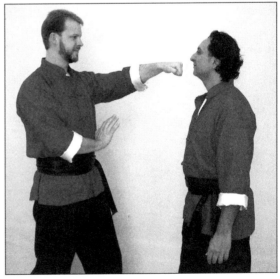

Half Fist

A half fist is slightly different than your standing striking punch. To accurately perform it, half twist your punch as it moves forward at your opponent. The strike should be completed once the thumb of the hand reaches the top. Remember to use only the striking knuckles of the index and middle fingers.

Teacup Strike

The structure of the teacup strike is used to extend all of the pressure of a punch straight through just the bones of your arm. To perform it, expose the outside of your wrist by bending your hand inward. Arc your arm in a swinging motion, being certain to only make contact with your opponent at the top, outside of your wrist. This strike may be used anywhere on your opponent's body and is usually used when finding your hand bent after blocking or sweeping an offense out of the way.

DO NOT ATTEMPT THIS STRIKE BY USING THE BACK OF YOUR HAND!

HYPEREXTENSION AND BREAKAGE WILL OCCUR!

Snake Strike

The snake fist is used to strike fast and hard. Lay your hand flat and palm down, making certain to raise it to eye level. This height will aid in better hitting your target. Using the tips of your fingers, jut your hand quickly forward, aiming for the eyes or throat of your opponent.

Talon

The talon is used to end a fight. Properly performed, it will completely restrict the airflow of your opponent's breathing. To perform IT, curl the pinky and ring finger of your hand inward toward your palm, exposing the middle, index, and thumb. Use these latter three by grabbing onto your opponent and attempting to touch the two fingers to your thumb, regardless of the flesh in between. This strike is best used upon the throat, but may be administered to other exposed muscle groups such as the side of the neck and triceps.

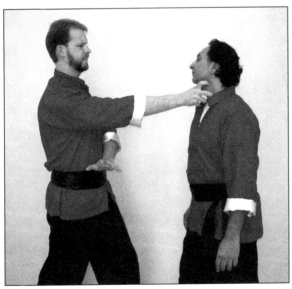

Tiger Claw

The tiger claw is as simple to perform as it seems. Bend the fingers of your striking hand until they are prepared to scratch at your opponent. This strike may be used on any fleshy area of your opponent's body.

Star Fist

This strike is used to land crushing, pressure point blows upon your opponent. Holding a closed fist, raise the knuckle of the middle finger slightly higher than the others. Swing the attack in an arced motion toward your opponent. This attack is recommended to be laid upon the temple, cheekbones, forehead, nose, and sternum of your opponent.

One never knows in advance which positioning an altercation will call for, so it is best to find fluency and versatility by regularly training each one of them. This practice is not as difficult or time consuming as one would imagine. An easy example would be found in considering the routine throwing of a basic strike. Each time, as you find your arm nearing the completion of the throw, quickly change the configuration of your hand to another setup, for example, from a palm strike to a half fist. Remember, the ability to quickly change your attack requires a greater amount of control. Therefore, you will be able to easily see your advancing expertise through the regular practice of these positions.

SECTION SIX
Kicking and Leg Movements

The importance of leg movements cannot be stressed enough. More than just holding you upright, leg movements alone can win or lose any altercation. You legs can both offer and exploit vulnerabilities with every action. Lower body attacks can also offer huge amounts of strength and extreme force. However, that opportunity demands responsibility. While these following attacks and movements will offer you unparalleled power, they come with a great price: your balance. Try to remember throughout this chapter that with every step or kick you take away half of your stability.

Proper Areas For Attacking With The Foot

As with every part of the body, there are certain areas that are more safe and useful to hit with than others. Below are two guides to illustrate and describe the best possible spots with which you may level a foot attack.

Bottom of the Foot

Just as was true with the underside of your hand, there are 3 very similar safe striking areas on the bottom of the foot.

1. Ball of the Foot

Just below the toes on the bottom of the foot you will find an area of padding. This area absorbs thousands of pounds of pressure every day through the simple act of walking and is hard enough to land a very powerful attack.

2. Side of the Foot/Knife Edge

The side of your foot of your foot allows for a sharp, direct manner with which you can land a kick. Thrown usually with a side kick, the knife edge can leave the same flat/sharp offense as an chop would.

3. Heel

The heel is the must durable surface you can level an attack with. You may your strike with as much force as you can muster without fear of injury. Make certain to only use the BOTTOM of the heal when striking and not the back of it.

THE TOES ARE NEVER TO BE USED! If you utilize your toes to land a kick you **WILL** break them.

Top of the Foot

The instep offers a very blunt debilitating strike to the side of the leg or knee. The proper striking area is just below the ankle on the top of the foot. Make certain to only level this attack on a "soft" area of the body or you may cause more harm to yourself with the kick.

Feel free to step on the foot of your assailant. As was true for us, so is true for them; the bones in the foot can be easily damaged if not guarded with the utmost care. This practice will not only injure the aforementioned bones and tendons of your attacker, but it will more importantly grossly limit their mobility and leave them open and vulnerable for a myriad of your following attacks.

Basic Kicking Techniques and Rules

Just as was important to recognize in placement of the hands and arms, so is true for the legs and feet. Too many times people focus their concentration on perfecting their upper body training and forget altogether the extreme importance of the lower body. All of our mobility, stability, and full body positioning are controlled by our legs, feet, and hips.

There are many techniques that can be used to advance our control over a confrontation. The absolute rules that surround these techniques are few and quite simple to understand.

First of all, unless moving, make certain to keep both feet on the ground. Any connection to the base (the floor) increases solidity and control. It only makes sense that it is better to have two supports preventing us from a hasty descent.

> Keep low; Lower than your opponent if possible. This is achieved by sinking your center by bending your knees to no more than the extent of your own personal comfort. When you attack at the inside or outside of your target's legs, you will have a stronger more readied foundation to act with.

Front Kick

A front kick offers you more choices on your style of attack. Whether using the direct pressure of the ball of your foot or the blunt force of your heel, the striking area can be the same. A frontal kick also incorporates the safety and opportunity of keeping your shoulders facing your opponent. Best results are found anywhere from the waist down.

Begin in a standard ready stance.

Raise your kicking leg first at the knee.

Finish your kick by laying the bottom of your foot upon your opponent's body.

Side Kick

A side kick offers power, precision, and range. The effects of a successfully laid kick can render an opponent completely incapacitated. As with all kicks, a standard side kick is best kept low, rising no higher than your opponent's waist. This lessens the possibility of having your foot or leg captured.

Begin in a standard ready stance.

Raise your kicking leg first at the knee.

Turn your hips to complete the strike, laying the side or "knife edge" of your foot on your opponent. This kick is well placed on the thigh, knee, or shin of your opponent.

Back Kick

Whereas the side kick is used for precision strikes, the back kick is utilized more for force and pressure attacks. The amount of strength in your legs reaches it's full potential when using this kicking style. For best results, this kick is aimed at the lower midsection of your attacker, remembering to keep your goal at or below the waist.

Begin in a standard ready stance.

Lift your kicking leg by the knee first.

Turn your hips full and extend your leg to complete this kick.

In & Out Kicks

In and out kicks are perfect for both training your body and use in an altercation. While they do teach your body mobility, balance, and proper usage of power, in and out kicks can also lay devastating blows on the upper legs of your attacker.

Begin in a standard ready stance.

Lift your kicking leg by the knee first.

Quickly twist your hips outward, leaving your instep to fall on the inside of your attacker's thigh.

The instant the first has landed, swivel your hips in the opposite direction and land another instep kick, this time on the outside of the same thigh.

Check Kick

Though they can be used in an offensive manner, check kicks are normally utilized more for defense. To perform an effective check kick, simply raise your foot as your opponent kicks and allow the pressure of that attack to be absorbed by the bottom of your foot. For best results, your foot should land upon the ankle or shin of the striking leg.

SECTION **SEVEN**
Beginning Combination Moves

For a long time there has been controversy over combinations of moves being taught together. While being a staunch proponent of never planning moves in advance, one must also admit that some things just fit together, planned or not. Consider move combinations as if you where going to the store. Instead of needing two strikes, you now need milk and bread. Ask yourself honestly if you would make two separate trips to your grocer or if you would simply buy them both at the same time. The analogy plays perfectly into the point. There is no reason that one always needs to reset before continuing. Sometimes an advantage is best maintained with paired movements that lead directly into one another.

Combinations of moves should not be considered dependent on each other, but rather held in mind as a series of individual movements; One technique that naturally leads into the next. After your first successful movement is spent, consider where your hand is. What else can you do from there? What has happened to your attacker as a result of your strike? Where do you need to position yourself next?

The following are illustrations of basic kung fu combination techniques. Each is a perfect example of how one movement, whether initially blocking or striking, can lead to a complete series of successful movements. Start slow and build these practices to a comfortable speed.

Rolling Fist Combinations

It is no coincidence that there are four standard blocks and a matching four rolling fist combinations. These series of movements were designed and are best used off of the basic blocking practices taught earlier in this book.

Upward Rolling Fist

Begin by using an upward block with your left hand.

Continue removing the strike by lifting the attacking elbow with your right hand.

Finish by striking your left palm against the now exposed ribcage of your attacker.

Inward Rolling Fist

Begin by pressing your right hand against the inside wrist of your attacker's right handed punch.

Transfer the control of the attacking inner wrist by lifting your left up from underneath.

Strike at your attacker's now exposed face with your right hand.

Outward Rolling Fist

Begin by pressing your left hand against the outside of your opponent's right handed punch.

Transfer the control of the attacking outer wrist by lifting it from underneath with your right.

Strike at your attacker's now exposed face with your left hand.

Downward Rolling Fist

Begin by pressing your left hand downward over your opponent's low right handed strike.

Continue by adding pressure to the elbow of the attacking arm with your right hand.

Finish the technique by striking your left hand at your opponent's now exposed face.

Kung Fu stylists make certain to keep both hands **continuously** moving during an attack. Yes, you may have completed a successful punch or kick, but what next? No fight is over until it is over completely and a conflict is almost never ended by one strike. The intention of this "key" is to state that once a successful blow has been landed, it is necessary to immediately follow it with another and another and another until the confrontation has been nullified. By continuously moving our hands, even during an attack, we allow ourselves much more opportunity for another strike to occur. Remember, an idle arm is not only a wasted option, but it can also be a target for our adversaries. The following "Triple set" is a perfect example of why this is equally important in striking practice. The control of rhythm is one aspect, but each hand, once pulled from it's striking position, next moves to perform a necessary block. The pattern of triple set creates a perfect blocking platform for the strikes it lays.

Triple Set

Triple set is an extremely effective pattern of blocks and strikes together. This system of movement not only fulfills the requirements of manipulating your opponent throughout multiple strikes, but also epitomizes the concept of efficiently moving based off of where your hands are. Triple set can be used on it's own or as finishing strikes to almost any attack. **Note: The darker arrow is the striking hand, the lighter represents the preparing hand.**

To start, draw your left hand back high and throw your right hand forward for a facial strike.

Next, draw your right hand down and back to your stomach and throw your left palm forward and high to hit at the very same spot.

Lastly, pull your left hand back to your right shoulder and jut your left out to strike at the ribcage of your opponent.

The strikes are high, high, low and only laid on one side. If you begin by striking the right side of your opponent's face, you must stay on that side, striking again at the right side of your opponent's face and lastly at the right ribcage. Below is a standard drill in which triple set can be utilized to finish an attack. **Remember to practice on both sides!**

Example of transfer to triple set attack

The beginning of the combination is upon the right handed punch of your attacker.

Start your defense with an inside rolling fist, commencing by pressing your right hand on the inside of the attacking wrist.

Transfer the control of the attacking inner wrist by lifting your left up from underneath.

Strike your right hand at the now exposed face of the attacker. (Note: This is now the first movement of your triple set).

132

Draw your right hand down and back to your stomach and throw
your left palm forward and high to hit at the very same spot.

Pull your left hand back to your right shoulder and jut your left
out to strike at the ribcage of your opponent.

Traveling Drill

Your opponent throws an attack at you.

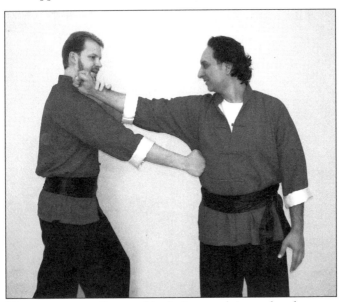

Using a return strike, you block the punch inward and away from you while throwing a strike of your own to the opponent's midsection with your right hand.

Once your first offense has been laid, you lift your right hand upward,
underneath your opponent's striking arm to prepare for further action.

Slide your right hand back to the wrist for more control.

Grab the wrist with your right hand.

Now free to act, throw your left palm at your opponent's face at the same time landing a check kick just over the closest knee.

Try not to hold the mindset of conquering your opponent with one well placed strike. Though it may be absolute at the moment, you should never rely on the success of your recently spent movements. Whether is necessary or not, you should always, always have another technique in bay waiting should it be needed. Never assume the confrontation is over until you can be UNDOUBTEDLY assured of that fact.

SECTION EIGHT
Solo & Paired Training Drills

One does not need to entirely change the manner in which they move to find perfect movement in Kung Fu, rather they only need to slightly alter their existing patterns. In this section of the book we shall discuss certain training patterns which will incorporate and enhance the existing structures with which we already react. Listed hereafter are several examples of simple regimens that will aid not only the practice of proper movement, but also help to remove the common physical mistakes.

In this section you must remember that you are rebuilding your body's reactions and as such you cannot expect to achieve expertise by simply understanding the idea of the movement; you must recreate your muscle memory. When beginning training drills it is always best to start slow and build up to a comfortable speed.

Here is a key for safety. It has been stated that if it hurts, don't do it, but sometimes lack of consideration betrays us. Stretching may reduce the risk of a muscle tear, but it will not make your body invincible against other self-inflicted injuries. Do not leave yourself short of a very important consideration. When training, FOLLOW THROUGH ON ALL MOVEMENTS. The strikes listed in this book are designed to provide **tremendous** damage to an adversary. By failing to complete the movement to fruition you are forcing the **entirety of that energy** to be absorbed by your own spine and other systems of joints as well. Pulling a punch is the same as retracting it's energy back into you. If a strike needs to be cut short, try instead to circle the energy around as outlined in this chapter.

Solo Drills

Remember the rules previously stated when practicing circles. Use your whole body in these drills, not just your arms. Allow yourself to yield the positive force of momentum, but always know, as your body draws energy in, so does it need to recycle that same energy out.

Forward Facing Circles

Begin your exercise with your arms outstretched and your wrists close to each other. Start a circular movement in one direction over your head and in front of you.

Continue the movement making certain to stay in same circular motion that you began with.

Cycle your energy over and over again until you feel the pattern and rhythm of your movement.

Lowering Side Circles

Begin this drill by drawing energy back toward you.

Once you have reached your chest, begin to cycle the force down in an arced motion.

Circle the force down in front of you.

Throw the force back to it's point of origin and repeat.

Rising Side Circles

Draw energy inward, this time bringing it in low to your waist.

Once you have reached your midsection, begin to arc and lift the force in front of you.

Cycle the energy upward and push it out from your chest.

Throw the entirety of the force to fall forward and back to it's point of origin and repeat.

Paired Drills

Paired drills are best thought of as training your body, not realistic fight scenarios. The drills listed below are repetitive and performed so that your body will react in a planned manner when needed. The desired effect is that we might remove the current threat and reset so that we are free to ready ourselves for any future course of events.

You need to have these movements become your default setting, even if you have exerted yourself a great deal. To do this: Practice regularly and relax during training. Try to expend as little energy as possible as you run your drills. If possible, train during fatigue to check accurate performance. Done properly, these techniques should not rely on strength whatsoever.

Clearing Drill

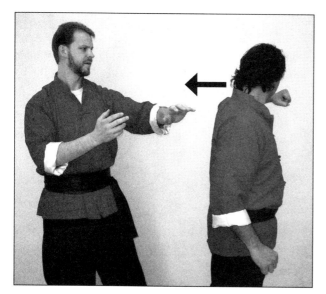

To begin have your partner stand with his/her back to you.
Once ready, have them throw a backfist to either side.

Stop the punch with a standard outward block, making sure
to bend the wrist outward as well for more control.

Once the force of the strike has been spent, remove the attack by pressing against your partner's elbow, "clearing" it with your free hand

The force of your "clear" should send your partner spinning in the opposite direction ready to make another backfist with the opposite hand.

Once again, block the strike with an outward block.

Once the force has been nullified, clear the attack.

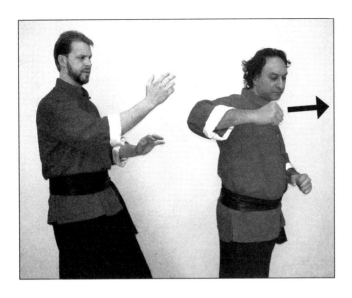

Ready yourself for your partner's continued movements.

This drill is best trained in series of ten strikes. This will not only aid against fatigue, but also allow you to switch places with your partner so that neither gets dizzy too quickly.

Clears are an integral part of Kung Fu. The concept of clears is that you should not attempt to do away with the complete force exerted by an opponent in one movement. Instead of trying to out-muscle a possibly stronger assailant, you may find yourself better off by simply stopping their attack with one motion and detaching it with another.

Mixed Rolling Drill

As is true with all others, this drill is to train into your muscle memory the practice of using multiple movements to rescind an opponent's strike. However with this practice, we find ourselves manipulating the attack against the attacker.

To begin, your partner throws a right handed punch at your face.

Block your punch with the left hand, pressing it inward, past you.

Raise your right hand from under both, transferring the
control you have over your partner's thrown hand.

Use your left hand to pin your partner's hand against their
body at the elbow.

Now it is your turn to throw the strike at your partner.

Using the very same pattern, your partner blocks your hand inward.

Next, your partner lifts his hand underneath both hands.

Allow your partner to then pin you at the elbow in the same manner.

As your partner throws his next punch, you have seen the pattern and are able to repeat...

by pressing inward against the strike.

Perform the mixed rolling drill over and over again on each side until your body is comfortable with the movement. In theory, the easy repeating of this one drill could go on without stop for hours. After much training, the efficiency of this technique will become second nature to you and lead your movement in any altercation.

The concept of constant contact: simply put, it is the idea that maintaining direct and unbroken physical contact with your opponent allows you not only to see how they are moving, but also to feel it. Reaction time can be cut down by half if this technique is applied properly. Even if blinded by some action during the confrontation, one will not be left indefensible. As is true with any training in Kung Fu, the more you practice it, the better you will be. The concept of constant contact is a perfect example of this fact.

By achieving and maintaining contact with your opponent, you will be able to sense the slightest alterations in your attacker's movement, thus giving you the edge. An example follows.

Paired Circles

Paired circles are used to practice recycling and redirecting energy without absorbing it.

Begin by matching both wrists with your partner in the "Chi Sau" position. Both right hands should be on the outside and both left on the inside.

Begin to accept the energy of your opponent as he presses down and into you.

157

As the force builds, start to angle the pressure, circling it downward.

Once the force has been removed from your direct path, begin to reissue it back in the direction of your partner.

Run through the cycle of motion as your return the same energy now back to your opponent.

Continue on as he lifts the energy and restart the drill.

Switch places regularly with your partner, making certain to play both parts of beginning and accepting the initial energy. Whether the instigator or the defender, both drills should be trained over and over again without stopping.

Paired Freestyle

Paired freestyle is the true essence of the concept of constant contact. There are no strikes in this drill, rather only trying to gently touch the opponent. The goal is to only practice guarding yourself by sensing the energy and movement of your partner as they move randomly around.

Begin in the standard Chi Sau position.

Commence movement with no preconceived notions or planned movement.

Continue the drill by yielding and accepting energy.

Summary

There it is. You now know the "secrets" and "magic" that every Kung Fu master relies upon. Always try to remember that it is this knowledge and not force that leads to expertise of the human body. As is true with any instrument you must practice to become fluent. Comfort in use of the movements will occur after time. As stated previously, eventually all of these techniques can become second nature to you, like sleepwalking.

Try to remember that it is not only the practice of positive movements that will make you an objective and active practitioner of Kung Fu, it is also and just as importantly the removal of bad practices that will make you a complete martial artist.

Remember to be patient, be relaxed, and be comfortable throughout your training. Hold in your mind the concept that you should not advance your training preemptively. Instead, your training will advance you when you are ready.

Training may be confusing at first, but consider that no one ever achieved their black sash overnight and neither did anyone without frustration. When the going gets tough, remember these three rules.

1. *Be patient.* Training takes a long time.

2. *Keep at it*, but take breaks when you need them.

3. *Never lose hope.* You can do this. There was a time when even walking was difficult for you. As was true for walking, so is true for Kung fu: With enough practice, anything can become easy.

About the Author

Sifu Noah Knapp has over 24 years experience in the martial arts. He has a 3rd degree black sash in Northern Drunken Style Kung Fu as well as training in Kenpo, Karate, Aikido, Kali, Silat & Tai Chi. He is a 2nd generation instructor at his family's kung fu school as well as an instructor for the STAR martial arts program. He has had the opportunity to advance his knowledge in real-life situations, serving as head of security and/or bouncer at many Los Angeles nightclubs including: The Playroom, A.D., The Gate, The Lounge and Balboa. You can contact him at sifunoah@yahoo.com.

Index

U

V

W

Y

Z